Published by Gluten-Free by Jan LLC

Gluten-Free by Jan LLC
16067 NW Rondos Dr.
Portland, OR USA 97229-9239

100 Tagalog Words for Children Copyright © 2026

ISBN: 979-8-9945334-1-3

100 TAGALOG

WORDS

FOR CHILDREN

Jeanette Withington
and
Edith Withington

Greetings & People

Hello - Kumusta
(koo-moos-tah)

Goodbye - Paalam
(pa-ah-lahm)

Thank you - Salamat
(sa-lah-mat)

Please - Pakiusap
(pa-ki-oo-sap)

Sorry - Paumanhin
(pa-oo-man-hin)

Hug - Yakap
(yah-kahp)

yes - Oo
(oh-oh)

No- Hindi
(hin-dee)

Me - Ako
(ah-ko)

We - Tayo
(tah-yoh)

You - Ikaw
(ee-kaw)

They - Sila
(see-lah)

Family & Friends

Mother - Nanay
(nah-nye)

Father - Tatay
(tah-tie)

Baby - Sanggol
(sung-gol)

Friend - Kaibigan
(kah-ee-bee-gan)

Grandma - Lola
(loh-la)

Grandpa - Lolo
(loh-lo)

Teacher - Guro
(goo-roh)

Sibling - Kapatid
(kah-pah-tid)

Nature

Sun - Araw
(ah-raw)

Moon - Buwan
(boo-wahn)

Star - Bituin
(bee-too-in)

Water - Tubig
(too-big)

Fire - Sunog
(soo-nog)

Sea - Dagat
(dah-gat)

Tree - Puno
(poo-no)

Flower - Bulaklak
(boo-lak-lak)

Animals

Dog - Aso
(ah-so)

Cat - Pusa
(poo-sah)

Bird - Ibon
(ee-bon)

Fish - Isda
(ees-dah)

Horse - Kabayo
(kah-bah-yo)

Elephant - Elepante
(eh-leh-panh-teh)

Tiger - Tigre
(tee-greh)

Snake - Ahas
(ah-has)

Places & Things

House - Bahay
(bah-hai)

School - Paaralan
(pah-ah-rah-lan)

Hospital - Ospital
(os-pee-tal)

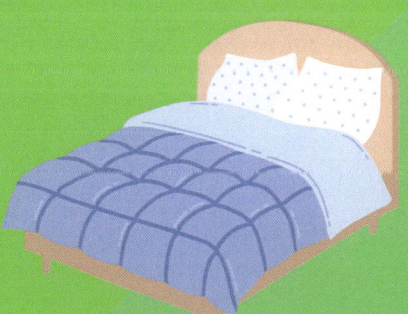

Bed - Kama
(kah-mah)

Chair - Upuan
(oo-poo-an)

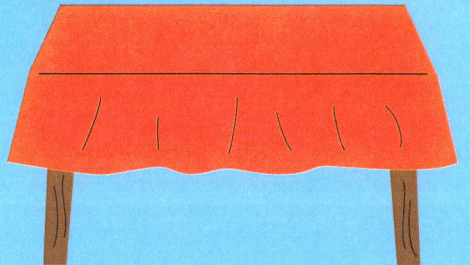

Table - Mesa
(meh-sah)

Car - Sasakyan
(sah-sak-yan)

Ball - Bola
(boh-lah)

Shoes - Sapatos
(sah-pah-tos)

Dress - Bestida
(beh-stee-dah)

Money- Pera
(peh-rah)

Book - Libro
(lee-broh)

Actions

Eat - Kumain
(koo-mah-in)

Drink - Inom
(ee-nom)

Sleep - Tulog
(too-lawg)

Walk - Lakad
(lah-kad)

Run - Takbo
(tahk-boh)

Jump - Lukso
(look-soh)

Play - Laro
(lah-roh)

Read - Basa
(bah-sah)

Colors

Red - Pula
(poo-lah)

Blue - Asul
(ah-sool)

Yellow - Dilaw
(dee-law)

Green - Berde
(behr-deh)

Black - Itim
(ee-teem)

White - Puti
(poo-tee)

Orange - Dalandan
(dah-lan-dahn)

Pink - Kulay Rosas
(koo-lahy roh-sahs)

Describing Words

Big - Malaki
(mah-lah-kee)

Small - Maliit
(mah-lee-it)

Hot - Mainit
(mah-ee-neet)

Cold - Malamig
(mah-lah-mig)

Happy - Masaya
(mah-sah-ya)

Sad - Malungkot
(mah-long-kot)

Fast - Mabilis
(mah-bee-lis)

Slow - Mabagal
(mah-bah-gahl)

Sweet

Sweet - Matamis
(mah-tah-mis)

Sour - Maasim
(mah-ah-sim)

Beautiful - Maganda
(mah-gahn-dah)

Handsome - Guapo
(gwah-po)

Numbers & Time

One - Isa
(ee-sah)

Two - Dalawa
(dah-lah-wah)

Three - Tatlo
(taht-loh)

Four - Apat
(ah-paht)

Five - Lima

(lee-mah)

Six - Anim

(ah-nim)

Seven - Pito

(pee-toh)

Eight - Walo

(wah-loh)

9

Nine - Siyam
(see-yahm)

10

Ten - Sampu
(sahm-poo)

AM

Morning - Umaga
(oo-mah-gah)

Night - Gabi
(gah-bee)

Directions

Here - Dito
(dee-toh)

There - Doon
(doh-on)

Up - Taas
(tah-as)

Down - Baba
(bah-bah)

Inside - Loob
(loh-ob)

Outside - Labas
(lah-bas)

Right - Kanan
(kah-nahn)

Left - Kaliwa
(kah-lee-wah)

Senses

See - Kita
(kee-tah)

Hear - Dinig
(dee-nig)

Taste - Lasa
(lah-sah)

Smell - Amoy
(ah-moy)

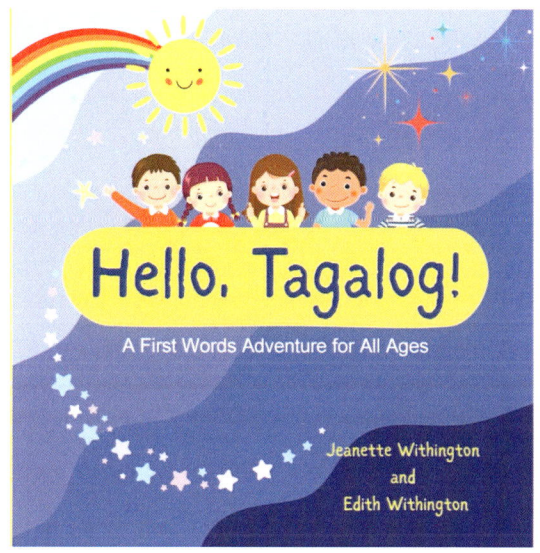

Explore more books by Jeanette Withington and Edith Withington